Somewhere In Between

A Spiritual Guide to Mentoring Young Men

Devin E. Caruthers

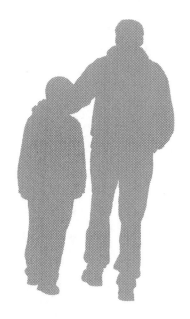

authorHOUSE®

AuthorHouse™
1663 Liberty Drive
Bloomington, IN 47403
www.authorhouse.com
Phone: 1-800-839-8640

First published by AuthorHouse 6/16/2011

ISBN: 978-1-4567-5530-0 (e)
ISBN: 978-1-4567-5531-7 (sc)

Library of Congress Control Number: 2011908045

Printed in the United States of America

Scripture quotations marked NIV are from the Holy Bible, New International
Version, copyright © 1973, 1978 The Zondervan Corporation

Scripture quotations marked KJV are taken from The Holy Bible, King James Version

"...If I had met you when I was 12, I might not be gay and I would have better grades in school...I would have had someone to make sure I stayed on track..."

-Anonymous

Table of Contents

The Need to Be Somewhere in Between viii

Why the title of the book? xii

Trevor xv

Chapter 1: Recognizing God's Voice 1

Marcus 10

Chapter 2: Patience 12

Allen 21

Chapter 3: Commitment 24

Isaiah 33

Chapter 4: Steel and Velvet 36

Paul 45

Chapter 5: A Naomi Reflection 48

Chapter 6: A Balance of Time 57

David 66

Chapter 7: Spiritually Aware 68

Getting Started 74

Scripture and Statement of Commitment 75

Addendum 76

Letters to My Father 77

      Letter #1 78

      Letter #2 80

      Letter #3 82

      Letter #4 84

      Letter #5 85

      "The Substitute" Preview 86

      The Substitute 87

About the Author 91

Religion that God our Father accepts as pure and faultless is this: to look after orphans and widows in their distress and to keep oneself from being polluted by the world.

James 1:27(NIV)

The Need to Be Somewhere in Between

Imagine you're eight-years-old living in the ghetto, in a borrowed house, on borrowed money. Your mother is a well-known customer to the streets and cannot stay sober or clean enough to raise you. You're raised by your grandmother who does her best to raise you right, but every now and then has her own setbacks. Your father? You are not sure who to call on because your mother conceived you incidentally in a transaction for a $10 hit of crack cocaine. Even at your young age, you are known to the block as "down," but to the school as a troublemaker. Neither school staff, the pastor at the neighborhood church, or the social worker can figure out why you display so much anger and aggression. The police know you and your family well because between your mother, uncles, aunts, and cousins, you have all earned jailhouse frequent flyer miles. Unfortunately, your family is your role model and serves as the blueprint to your future. You have an avid love for the streets and all of the iniquities thereof because they validate you. Your frequent outbreaks of violence and anger are icons for the streets and they love you for it. You are absent of hope, apathetic to education, and hold no respect for anything lawful or positive. After nine years of school suspensions, alcohol consumption, drug use, and petty crime, your streets let you down. You find yourself facing 10 years in prison for armed criminal action-which you committed while attempting to rob an elderly man for a few dollars. You are now seventeen years old with no education, and bound for a decade where all you will learn is how to be a better criminal.

The story of the life of this young man is not only true, but it is a far too familiar depiction of the situations and circumstances that are occurring daily across America. No longer does the modern day family consist of a husband, wife, two kids, and a dog. In today's times, the family is a combination of parents, grandparents, and guardians who are all grappling to hang on and keep each other from failing. What is the cause of the failure of families today? The family has lost its primary foundation, the father, which is the cornerstone of its existence and success. The father is absent, and generation after generation is growing up without him in a time where he is needed most.

Fathers are often found out of position, missing in action, or absent without leave. Instead of taking their position at the head of the family, they are found in the streets, prisons, with another family, or often times are not found at all. Due to the lack of their proper positioning, the outlook for the children who are left behind is bleak. Children today are often referred to as a "lost generation." On the contrary, if you consider the fact the God ordained the father as the head of the family and if he has left his position, the children of today are actually a "left generation." Fathers have left their boys and forced them to learn how to be men through watching the behaviors of music artists and sports figures, forcing them to adopt their negative characteristics. They have left their sons with no other choice but to figure out how to help their mother raise their siblings and figure out how to keep food on the table. They are also left to make the decision of whether or not to have pre-martial sex, which can result in conceiving children themselves and unconsciously modeling their father's behavior by not caring for their own.

Throughout the course of time, life has had a way of repositioning itself to adjust or adapt to a new condition or environment. In general, mankind instinctively adapts to the changes in the condition of its environment therefore making survival possible. In this same manner, the men of God, like you, who understand the plight of young men, must reposition themselves to fill the gap that the natural father has left. You must be willing and able to take the place of the fathers who have abandoned their children and assume the role of "father." If you should have the tenacity and the desire to stand in such a position, you should be fully prepared for the enormous task ahead. It certainly does not come without significant doses of frustration, feelings of inadequacy, and emotional exhaustion. Although these things are inevitable, you must understand that the intensity of your passion must be great to bring about a positive change in the lives of the young men whom you will influence.

In order to learn how to stand "Somewhere in Between," men must position themselves as fathers and possess seven key attributes:

1. Ability to recognize God's voice
2. Patience
3. Exemplify exceptional commitment
4. Be Steel and Velvet
5. Display a Naomi reflection
6. Ablity to effectively balance time
7. Possess spiritual awareness

When these attributes are possessed and exercised, the "left" generation of young men will have a chance at success and have a great opportunity to reverse the cycle that is plaguing society. It is my desire that all who read this book understand the need for a spiritual approach to mentorship that requires an intense and personal commitment to God's purpose.

Why the title of the book?

In the sixth chapter of John, there is a story told about a miracle that Jesus performed by feeding 5000 people with two fish and five loaves of bread. Many have read or heard this story, but many miss the significant origin of the bread and fish. In the story, the young boy had these portions with him, and you can perhaps speculate that he was carrying his lunch planning to hear Jesus preach. I imagine that when he left his house that morning, he had no idea that his small lunch would be used in a great miracle.

Some of the disciples who were with Jesus noticed the boy and pointed him out to Jesus. Who knew that a young boy, who the people did not know, would be used by God in such a great way? How often do you see our young men standing around you with no father to help them use what they have? You often overlook them and fail to help them reach their full potential. I imagine this young boy didn't have a prominent family name, wasn't dressed in fancy clothes, and wasn't rich, but instead was a peasant from a poor village. Yet, Jesus stepped "somewhere in between" and used what the boy had to the glory of His father in heaven.

Many young men walk through life and have no idea of the potential that they carry with them. Many of them need someone that is willing to be *somewhere in between* and help them realize their potential. Just like the young boy, many young men don't come from notable families or rich homes, but all carry an unexpected miracle around with them every day. The miracles are not always instantly recognizable, but with the help of someone who is *somewhere in between*, miracles can happen. It doesn't take much to ignite the potential within, but someone has to be willing to show them what they carry. To be *somewhere in between* means to be whatever you have to be for each young man. It means that you're willing to take them as they are, broken and all, and treat them as your own son. Jesus could have very well ignored the young boy who had nothing to offer but two fish and five loaves of bread. He could have looked at His own situation, the need to feed many, and dismiss the boy who could only feed one. Instead, Jesus looked at the potential of the meal and the boy's willingness to share, instead of the obstacles that seem to stand in the way. Young men want someone with whom they can share their life, their dreams, and their potential miracles. It is up to you as a mentor to put yourself in a position of being *somewhere in between* so that you can see the potential instead of the obstacles. To truly be effective, you have to be more than a mentor. You have to be more than someone that pops in and out at your convenience. It is never convenient to be *somewhere in between* but it is necessary. Somewhere In Between is not only an effective guide to mentoring, it is mentoring God's way.

"My sheep listen to my voice; I know them, and they follow me." – John 10:25-27 (NIV)

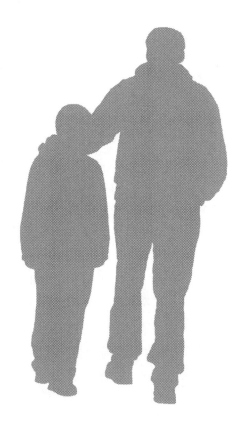

Trevor

It was a hot and humid summer day in June and I was attending a track meet for my godson. There were thousands of participants and spectators in the stands and lining the sides of the track. While waiting for my godson's next event, I noticed a young man who looked familiar to me. I couldn't recall where I had seen him, but was sure I had seen him before. I dismissed the thought and continued to watch the meet and socialize with other parents. A few minutes later, I again saw this kid and this time had the feeling that I needed to go talk to him. At that moment, I recalled that maybe I had seen him at track practice one day a few months prior where my wife was the head coach. I sent her a text message describing this young man in an attempt to verify where I had seen him. She immediately confirmed that this was most likely Trevor, who did indeed run for her that previous spring.

As the meet went on, I again had a feeling that I needed to talk to Trevor. This time the feeling was much stronger. I was hesitant to talk to him because I didn't know this kid nor did I see any reason to talk to him. The more I kept ignoring the feeling, the stronger it became. A short while later, I entered the restroom and to my surprise, Trevor came in to use the restroom too! Finally, I surrendered to the Holy Spirit, and as we exited the restroom, I introduced myself.

It wasn't until later that day that I realized it was the Holy Spirit that was speaking to me. It actually began months prior, when God simply planted the seed for what He would assign me to do sometime later. God had me at the right place and right time months prior. I left work early one day and stopped by to see my wife to watch her track practice. It was there that I first saw Trevor, but never talked to him or even knew his name. God kept his image in my memory knowing that I would run across him again at a track meet and He had an assignment for me.

In only 18 months time, I went from a stranger to Trevor to his godfather and close friend to his family. I recognized God's voice and obeyed His command and I have helped Trevor through many situations. I have also been there for him both physically and emotionally. I have allowed God to use me in a miraculous way simply because I listened to His voice that hot, summer day. I sometimes wonder what may have become of Trevor if I had not listened to God. What an opportunity I may have missed to know Him and be a part of his life. I am thankful to God for the opportunities to serve Him in such a great way.

Chapter 1: Recognizing God's Voice

I have a vivid memory of the events leading up to me recognizing the voice of God for the first time. It was a spring afternoon during my college years and I was on my way to campus to study; this day I decided to take an alternate route. I began to pass an elementary school when I saw an old friend that I knew from back home. He was on the basketball court coaching a group of young kids. It had been some time since I had seen him, so I turned around to speak with him and catch up on old times. As we talked, he informed me that the school had just started a basketball team and he needed help coaching. I was in my last semester of school and was preparing for finals so I was reluctant to agree to assist him. During that practice, one of the players approached me with a pleasant grin and asked if I was going to be his coach. Before I had a chance to answer, he introduced himself and assured me he was the best player on the court. He disappeared down court, and right after practice he was down the block headed home. Before leaving, I talked to my friend again who told me that the young man that I met needed some guidance. His parents were addicted to crack cocaine, his father was always in and out of prison, and he was often in trouble at school.

Reluctantly, I agreed to assist him and coach the basketball team. I went home that evening wondering why I had committed to this, which I knew I didn't have time for and even thought about backing out of the commitment. Although my schedule was tight, something kept drawing me to that court. Everyday, at each practice, that young man was there, and I felt a strong need to keep coming; so I did. After a short time, that young man from the court often appeared on my apartment steps waiting until I arrived home. By this time, I had met his brother as well, and both quickly bonded with me and desired to be with me wherever I went. One evening, while at the store, they both approached me and wanted to ask a question. They asked if I could be their godfather. Taken aback by such a grand request, I asked if they realized what they were asking of me. Both nodded and explained that it meant if their parents could not care for them, then they would stay with me. At first, I figured they were speaking without realizing the seriousness of the question and started to dismiss it; however, after pausing a moment, making sure to select my response carefully, I turned and looked at them, but I didn't see *them*. It was at that moment that God spoke to my spirit and told me that it was *His* will that I be in their lives. The fear of such a commitment rippled through me and I stood in the aisle speechless.

I said "yes" that day, not to the request of the two boys, but to the command of God. He had prepared me for the question since that first day on the court. It was not by coincidence that I went a different way to campus that day. God placed me at the right place and perfect time to lead me to fulfill His ultimate purpose: to become *somewhere in between* for these boys (Romans 8:28). It was that day that He started me on a journey to encourage, motivate, and cause positive disruption in the lives of young men as He placed them in my path.

The key to positioning yourself in the life of another is to simply recognize God's voice. If I hadn't recognized it, then I would have missed the divine assignment to be used by God, and those two boys would have missed a greater opportunity: to know God. God will use you if you are willing to be *somewhere in between* as a cornerstone in His ministry. He will empower you to teach, guide, and support His sons who are left alone in a world that is hard and unforgiving.

How do you recognize God's voice?

In John 10:27, Jesus communicates the essential requirement necessary to hear what God has to say to you. In this scripture, Jesus is speaking at the Feast of Dedication in Jerusalem. While walking in Solomon's Colonnade, He is questioned by a crowd of unbelieving Jews who desire more evidence that He actually is the Christ. They requested if Jesus was the Christ, that He tell them plainly.

Jesus answered, "I did tell you, but you do not believe. The miracles I do in my Father's name speak for me, but you do not believe because you are not my sheep. My sheep listen to my voice; I know them, and they follow me." – John 10:25-27 (NIV)

The words that Jesus spoke in the Colonnade still apply to you today. In order for you to listen to God's voice, you must first be His sheep. In order to become His sheep, you must accept Jesus Christ as your Lord and Savior. It is then that your heart becomes open to hear the voice of God and you can begin to know God and follow His commands. Several times in the Bible, Jesus often compares His children to sheep. As many times as I have read some of those passages, it was not until sometime later that the Holy Spirit challenged me to discover *why* we are referred to as sheep. When this truth was revealed to me, it then taught me how to respond to God's command and encouraged me to be *somewhere in between* in the lives of young men.

How do you respond to God's command?

It is by no coincidence that God uses the characteristics of sheep as a comparison to His children that follow Him. In both ancient and modern religious rituals, sheep were often used as sacrificial animals. Likewise, when God sent His son, the sacrificial lamb, Jesus Christ, to die for mankind's inequity, He became a sacrifice just like a sheep.

"He was oppressed and afflicted, yet he did not open his mouth; he was led like a lamb to the slaughter, and as a sheep before her shearers is silent, so he did not open his mouth."
Isaiah 53:7(NIV)

If you recognize that you are like a sheep, you can accept that Jesus Christ is your Shepherd, the leader of His flock. Without Him, you cannot know the way to eternal life and will never reach your full potential in your mortal life. I found myself in a situation where I heard what God said, but struggled with how to respond to His command. At a very critical point in my life, God commanded me to take in a young man and be everything to him that a father should be. However, I was recently married and had just experienced the birth of my first child. How at such a time in my life as this could God ask me to sacrifice so much?

The answer lies in our level of faith. The Bible speaks much about faith (Hebrews 11:1). By questioning if I would be able to fulfill my duties as a husband and new father, while taking on another child as my son, I actually doubted what God could do. Many times in your life doubt is what prevents you from becoming what God would have you to be and ultimately fulfilling your purpose. You live your life questioning tomorrow and doubting your direction. It is at the lowest and most difficult times in your life when God tests your faith level by asking you to do the unreasonable, the unimaginable, and the illogical. God's testing of faith level reminds me of the widow woman from Zarephath that the prophet Elijah met. The Bible teaches that at this time there was a famine going on across the region, but God had a plan and He sent Elijah on a special assignment.

"Some time later the brook dried up because there had been no rain in the land. Then the word of the LORD came to him: "Go at once to Zarephath of Sidon and stay there. I have commanded a widow in that place to supply you with food." So he went to Zarephath. When he came to the town gate, a widow was there gathering sticks. He called to her and asked, "Would you bring me a little water in a jar so I may have a drink?" As she was going to get it, he called, "And bring me, please, a piece of bread."

"As surely as the LORD your God lives," she replied, "I don't have any bread—only a handful of flour in a jar and a little oil in a jug. I am gathering a few sticks to take home and make a meal for myself and my son, that we may eat it—and die."

Elijah said to her, "Don't be afraid. Go home and do as you have said. But first make a small cake of bread for me from what you have and bring it to me, and then make something for yourself and your son. [14] *For this is what the LORD, the God of Israel, says: 'The jar of flour will not be used up and the jug of oil will not run dry until the day the LORD gives rain on the land.' "*

She went away and did as Elijah had told her. So there was food every day for Elijah and for the woman and her family. For the jar of flour was not used up and the jug of oil did not run dry, in keeping with the word of the LORD spoken by Elijah. – I Kings 17:7-15 (NIV)

Responding to God's command with the faith of the widow woman will place you in position to become strong mentors, youth leaders, and fathers to all those whom God places in your path. Just as God fed the widow, Elijah and her son, so too did He bless me and my house simply because I was obedient and responsive to His command.

Points to Consider

Chapter 1: Recognizing God's Voice

- Recognizing God's voice requires that you are His sheep
- Responding to God's command places you in position to fulfill His purpose
- God blesses you based on your faith level

Somewhere to Write...

How has God spoken to you since you began reading this book? How did you respond? How has listening to God's voice benefited your mentoring experience?

_____

_____

_____

_____

_____

_____

_____

_____

_____

_____

_____

_____

_____

_____

_____

_____

_____

_____

_____

Somewhere to Write...

_____

_____

_____

_____

_____

_____

_____

_____

_____

_____

_____

_____

_____

_____

_____

_____

_____

_____

_____

_____

_____

_____

"But that on the good ground are they, which in an honest and good heart, having heard the word, keep it, and bring forth fruit with patience".
Luke 8:15 (KJV)

Marcus

Marcus presented a completely new challenge for me. He was by far the most rebellious and selfish of all of those who God had placed in my life. Marcus never asked me to be there, nor did he want me there most of the time. At 13-years-old, he had already grown up to be very selfish, and unless there was some benefit to him, he rarely did anything for anyone. My commitment to my assigned journey God had me on was deeply challenged by my experience with Marcus. His personality was one that rubbed most people the wrong way. He had few friends and didn't seem to be able to maintain any of the friendships he did have. At some point I asked God why he made me available for someone who was so hard-headed, disrespectful, self-centered, and didn't want me guiding or teaching him anything. God quietly reminded me that my commitment to standing *somewhere in between* was not dependant on Marcus's treatment of me; rather it was about my commitment to *Him*.

Like most of those I cared for, Marcus lived in a single parent home where his mother was the primary caregiver. His father, although he lived in town, decided when Marcus was 13-years-old that he couldn't be a father to him any longer for his personal reasons. Marcus had difficulty accepting this tribulation because his father was in his life for most of his childhood, and they once had a good relationship. My presence only angered him because he viewed my involvement as an attempt to replace his father. Although I continued to be involved, it was a year-and-a half later before he decided to accept me into his life.

The greatest lesson I learned through my experience with Marcus was patience. He often neglected to take care of his responsibilities and was immature, rebellious, selfish, and ungrateful. There were so many times that Marcus pushed me away. Although I supported him in various ways including purchasing school clothes, caring for him when he was sick, and paying for his cell phone, I was often treated as an insignificant part of his life. Father's Day would come and go and I rarely received any recognition. My birthday would pass and I would only get a text message. Even at Christmas, Marcus always was expecting to receive, but never ready to give.

The love of God in me caused me to be patient with Marcus. I prayed for him often and loved him despite his faults. As time went on, I did see growth within him and our relationship grew stronger. There were several issues I was able to help Marcus through because I refused to give up. I refused to let go and walk away regardless of how difficult the relationship became. I trusted God and patiently continued to stand *somewhere in between*.

Chapter 2: Patience

There is a special place in the heart of all men that is considered "precious real estate." The vastness of this space depends on the life and character of the one to which it belongs. Whether it is wide open and flat or small and mountainous, it is an exclusive area that is held only for that most regarded individual; the natural father. It is the natural father of boys who has hold of this special area of the heart. The inner soul of the male considers their "real" father as the source of his very existence. It is the instinctive natural drive within men that controls their desire to be close to him. They look to their natural father to identify who they are and who they might become. Our natural father holds the key to their talents, strengths, and even weaknesses. Men often look to him to be the model they use as they grow into manhood (Proverbs 8:17:6); however, the fallacy in this occurs when the natural father is not present and active in their lives and/or is not a positive influence. If it is by his example and presence that boys learn how to grow into men, then what do they become without him?

In a society where a present and dedicated father is rare, the hearts of his children still seek him. They still long for him whether the interaction is positive or negative. I recall meeting a young man who was 14-years-old. He lost his father to homicide and his mother to a car accident both within a year. He was five-years-old at the time of the tragedies and since that time lived with his grandparents. He often found himself in trouble at school because of fighting, cutting class, and showing disrespect toward virtually every adult. God placed this child in my path and I begin interacting with him on a bi-weekly basis. The next year proved to be a great challenge as I came to know him and he came to know me.

I often found myself answering phone calls or emails from teachers reporting that he was not doing what he was asked or that his grades were low. A significant amount of time, love, and encouragement was poured into this young man and he showed signs of improvement from time to time. Anytime that he got in trouble and I stepped in to hand down a consequence or punishment, I was commonly met with attitude, frustration, and resentment. This was driven by the overwhelming fact that I was not his father. I found myself in a conflict of position. In actuality, he was correct; I was not his father. I was simply attempting to stand in the gap. Why was I met with such opposition? His father was not living and could be in position. I soon realized that I was on "private property" in the area of the heart of this young man that he refused to sell or lease, but would only allow me an occasional visit. My attempt to be in position as his father was one of good intentions, but was not well-received.

As you strive to fit *somewhere in between*, you must realize the preciousness of this area on which you trod. You have to be careful not to disrespect it, but take the time to understand it. It is necessary to find a good balance between discipline, guidance, nurturance, and friendship so you are not asked to vacate the premises. As leaders, you must be able to reach beyond the secular world and become spiritual leaders for these young men. You must teach and guide them along their journey and learn how to influence them and lead them in the positive direction that God would have them to go. It is crucial, however, to not reveal to them that they are being led. In this way, you avoid the common characteristic of human nature, which is to rebel against things simply for the sake of rebellion.

How do you enter the heart and make a place there? First, you must make some hard, challenging assumptions. You must assume that you will be met with opposition and will have to be aggressive in your approach, yet velvet in your methods. In other words, mentor with purpose. Be open and honest about your goals of the relationship. Be direct, yet find your way into their heart with finesse. I once told a young man, whom I now have accepted as my son, that if his natural father did not choose to be involved, that I would do what was necessary and stand in his place. I was deliberate in my intentions and clear about my motives. I let him know that everything I would soon do was for his benefit and I did it because he was worth my time, effort, and sacrifice. I did not ask if he minded if I looked after him, I simply started working. I took him upon my shoulders and worked along side his mother to help her see to his needs. I assumed a role as his father, that was not always appreciated or welcomed, but I stayed committed to him and asked God to give me patience. I was able to look beyond the moment and see the ultimate goal. I had to teach him about manhood, I had to support his education, and I had to guide him spiritually. I was consistently there for him whether it was in the stands at sporting events, at parent-teacher conferences, at his bedside when he was sick, or there to hold him at times when he was crying. I was able to win his favor as well as his trust.

You must always remember that all things happen in God's time, not your own. You must have patience and realize that you are working for His divine glory and ultimately for His purpose. I am reminded of the parable Jesus spoke about the sower regarding patience:

A farmer went out to sow his seed. As he was scattering the seed, some fell along the path; it was trampled on, and the birds of the air ate it up. Some fell on rock, and when it came up, the plants withered because they had no moisture. Other seed fell among thorns, which grew up with it and choked the plants. Still other seed fell on good soil. It came up and yielded a crop, a hundred times more than was sown."
Now the parable is this: The seed is the word of God. Those by the way side are they that hear; then cometh the devil, and taketh away the word out of their hearts, lest they should believe and be saved. They on the rock are they, which, when they hear, receive the word with joy; and these have no root, which for a while believe, and in time of temptation fall away. And that which fell among thorns are they, which, when they have heard, go forth, and are choked with cares and riches and pleasures of this life, and bring no fruit to perfection. But that on the good ground are they, which in an honest and good heart, having heard the word, keep it, and bring forth fruit with patience.
Luke 8:5-8, 12-15(KJV)

As an analogy to this parable, you are the farmer and the seed is the Word of God. The young men God sends your way are in every one of the places mentioned in the parable; the path, the rock and among thorns. As God's farmers, you must make sure these young men are placed on good soil. If you are willing to sow seeds in the lives of the young men whom God places before you, you will produce forceful and positive men of God who will be positive leaders in their families, churches, and communities. You who are willing to be patient and who always trust and depend on God will be useful tools in His ministry. You must be patient through resentful and disrespectful moments, immature behavior, undeveloped spiritual growth, and ungrateful attitudes, never giving up on the ultimate goal (Galatians 6:9). You must always focus on the ultimate goal of God and understand that it is by His grace through faith that you are saved and you are able to stand as leaders in His ministry.

For by grace you have been saved through faith, and that not of yourselves; it is the gift of God,[9] not of works, lest anyone should boast. For we are His workmanship, created in Christ Jesus for good works, which God prepared beforehand that we should walk in them.
Ephesians 2:8-9 (NIV)

Points to Consider

Chapter 2: Patience

- Find a balance between discipline, guidance, nurturance, and friendship
- Assume opposition will be met and the approach will have to be aggressive and the methods velvet
- Be patient through disrespect, resentment, immature behavior, undeveloped spiritual growth and ungrateful attitudes

Somewhere to Write...

Reflect on a time when mentoring tested your patience. How did you handle it? After reading this chapter, how would you now handle that situation?

_____

_____

_____

_____

_____

_____

_____

_____

_____

_____

_____

_____

_____

_____

_____

_____

_____

Somewhere to Write...

_____

_____

_____

_____

_____

_____

_____

_____

_____

_____

_____

_____

_____

_____

_____

_____

_____

_____

_____

_____

_____

_____

Isaac spoke up and said to his father
Abraham, "Father?"
"Yes, my son?" Abraham replied.
"The fire and wood are here," Isaac said, "but
where is the lamb for the burnt offering?"
Genesis 22:7(NIV)

Allen

Allen was at the start of *somewhere in between*. He was 9-years-old when God brought him into my life. I was a 22-year-old college student in my fourth year. While working my part-time job as a substitute teacher at an elementary school, a teacher approached me and asked if I was interested in mentoring a young man who was troubled. Eventually I met Allen and his grandmother who was very excited about the thought of me getting involved with her grandson. I soon learned that Allen was born from a prostitute mother who was addicted to crack cocaine and an unknown father. Most of his aunts and uncles were either in prison or had been, and Allen was on his way to the same fate fast. This was indeed my first experience standing *somewhere in between* and I wasn't quite sure which way to go or what decisions to make. I soon found out that God used Allen for my training, and this experience set in motion the pursuit of God's purpose for my life.

Allen was thought of by most as a very handsome young man. He had a smile that could light up a room and a unique laugh that was contagious. His eyes were adorable to women who would always comment on them and make him blush with embarrassment. He always came across to strangers as a sweet and respectful child, but Allen had a darker side that it didn't take too long for me to see. He would often have fits of rage, even to the point of one night grabbing a knife from my kitchen and attempting to cut himself simply because he couldn't ride his bike. Once out of control, Allen had to be physically restrained to prevent him from harming himself or destroying property. He was constantly kicked out of school and even at 9-years-old often ran away from home to avoid discipline. Due to his behavior, Allen had no friends. For his 10th birthday, his grandmother and I threw him a birthday party and invited all of his classmates. No one showed. He was devastated, although he never admitted it. Although he looked to me as "father," even I didn't always get along with him. His behavior was so erratic that I was often guarded, never knowing what mood or behavior to expect. I often wondered why God had me in his life, especially since I was a busy college student who really didn't have time to spend outside of my studies. I was not spiritually mature enough to make the connection to God's will for my life. That did not come until years later.

After a year working with Allen, it seemed like nothing I was doing had any effect. He still got in trouble at school and home, and his emotional instability didn't seem to change. I felt as though I wasn't helping him. I remember sitting on my couch one evening and I began to cry. I couldn't believe I was actually crying over this child who wasn't my own, but I realize now it was God creating a compassionate heart within me, which was necessary for the purpose He had for my life.

Years later, after I graduated from college and moved back to my hometown, I did my best to keep in touch with Allen and encourage him from a distance. Unfortunately, one night he decided to rob an elderly man at gunpoint and assaulted him before he fled. He was caught, charged, and convicted of armed robbery and armed criminal action at the age of 16. He was sentenced to 8 years in prison; one in juvenile detention and the other seven would be served in an adult penitentiary. Even as I write this book, Allen is still serving his sentence. I often wonder how he's doing, and if he ever thinks of me. I also wonder when he's released if all that I taught him will be remembered. Although Allen's outcome wasn't good, I learned a great deal through my experience with him. God taught me to be committed to His purpose even when the outcome was not what I desired. I have used those lessons to continue to stand *somewhere in between* in the lives of others.

Chapter 3: Commitment

What is it within the hearts and minds of men that causes personal disregard for self? How can you become able to look beyond the trees and see the forest? Once you have learned how to recognize God's voice and have learned how to exercise patience, you can achieve a higher level of commitment to do the work that God has for you. It is extremely difficult to stand *somewhere in between* while enduring other stresses in life. One of the most challenging things you will face is remaining committed to these young men through moments of disrespect, resentment, ingratitude, and selfishness. How do you keep striving? How do you stay involved? Ultimately, how do you remain committed?

As God moved me through this process, there were countless times that I wanted to walk away. It was indeed hard to spend so much time, money, and effort pouring my heart and soul into the lives of others when met with opposition. It seemed that no matter what, something happened that caused considerable emotional stress and discontentment. I vividly recall a time where God decided to develop my commitment to Him and to what He had me doing. It was a challenging time in my marriage where my wife had endured all that she could and handed me an ultimatum. She demanded that either things changed or she and our son would leave. She loved me very much, and I equally loved her, but God handed me a burden that I didn't think I could bear. He had me standing *somewhere in between* striving to be a husband, a father, a coach, and a youth leader, and I struggled to stay committed. I had worked so hard to bring these young men into my life and strived to set the example of a proper "family" and a Godly marriage so that they could one day model after it in their own relationships. How ironic that the very thing I was trying to accomplish by bringing them into my life was on the verge of crashing down around me. If my marriage failed, how was I going to explain it to these boys? How could I continue as a single parent? The position of "father" in the family was the whole premise for what God had called me to do. How was I to explain to God my failure? It was tough to be on a journey with a set destination that God has only shared with you. How could I get my wife to see the importance of my position? How long would she hang on? This wasn't her version of "happily ever after." I was unaware that God had already spoken to my wife's heart. He reminded me of how He sent His angel to speak to Joseph regarding Mary's pregnancy with Jesus. Consider this text:

But after he had considered this, an angel of the Lord appeared to him in a dream and said, "Joseph son of David, do not be afraid to take Mary home as your wife, because what is conceived in her is from the Holy Spirit. Matthew 1:20 (NIV)

Just as God commanded the angel to speak to Mary, He commanded the Holy Spirit to speak to my wife. He revealed to her that I truly was following the direction of God and that what I was doing was purely His will.

How awesome it is that in all things you endure and experience, God provides an answer through His Word. I was concerned with how I could convince my wife that this was what God wanted me to do. Over a period of several years, God continually tested my commitment to His purpose. Once I proved that I could recognize His voice and practice patience, only then did He speak to my wife and reveal to her that this ministry was what He ordained. I remained committed to God's direction for my life and He honored my commitment by giving my wife understanding and acceptance. I often asked myself, why the test? God gave me the answer in James 1:2-4 (NIV):

Consider it pure joy my brothers, whenever you face trials of many kinds, because you know that the testing of your faith develops perseverance. Perseverance must finish its work so that you may be mature and complete, not lacking anything.

If I did not believe in what God was doing though me, my heart could not persevere and my commitment would falter. I had to show God and prove to myself that no matter what God asked me to do; I would follow Him, even if it meant sacrificing the things that I cherished most in my life.

You who are committed to His purpose will have to face trials of many kinds and will be tested to prove that commitment and faith. I am reminded of Abraham who proved his great faith and commitment to God that day on a mountain in Moriah. Abraham's journey with his son Isaac is symbolic of standing *somewhere in between.*

Isaac, and he himself carried the fire and the knife. As the two of them went on together, ⁷ Isaac spoke up and said to his father Abraham, "Father?"
"Yes, my son?" Abraham replied.
"The fire and wood are here," Isaac said, "but where is the lamb for the burnt offering?"

⁸ Abraham answered, "God himself will provide the lamb for the burnt offering, my son." And the two of them went on together. Genesis 22:6-8 (NIV)

I'm certain that it was with great turmoil and anguish that Abraham made the journey up the mountain that day. The Bible teaches that God commanded Abraham to sacrifice his son by killing him on the mountain. Isaac was Abraham's only child and one with whom God blessed Abraham and his wife Sarah with in their old age. This was a seemingly impossible request that God made of Abraham. He had to put aside his own desires, goals, and needs simply because God commanded him to do so. Abraham had already witnessed God do so many other things in his life and he refused to question God's plan.

Standing *somewhere in between* requires the same great commitment and sacrifice as demonstrated by Abraham. My family, money, health, and all that I had was given to me by God, just as Isaac was given to Abraham. Often times God will ask you to go up a mountain and sacrifice the "Isaacs" in your life for His eternal purpose. I had to believe God, put aside my own agenda, and trust His wisdom. The benefits of doing so, however, are immeasurable. As you stand in commitment to God, He will direct your path (Proverbs 3:5) and give you great opportunity in His ministry.

Points to Consider

Chapter 3: Commitment

- God will honor your commitment to Him by bringing understanding to those around you
- Unless you believe in the work that God is doing, your commitment will falter
- Put aside your own agenda and trust God's wisdom

Somewhere to Write...

How committed are you to God's children? Has God ever given you an Abraham experience as he did with his son Isaac? How did you respond?

_____

_____

_____

_____

_____

_____

_____

_____

_____

_____

_____

_____

_____

_____

_____

_____

_____

_____

_____

Somewhere to Write...

Somewhere to Write...

"My son,' the father said, 'you are always with me, and everything I have is yours. But we had to celebrate and be glad, because this brother of yours was dead and is alive again; he was lost and is found." – Luke 15:31-32 (NIV)

Isaiah

Isaiah was one that required the most discipline, yet he was also the one with whom I had the closet relationship. I set expectations and put rules in place, and I could always count on Isaiah to test them. He took me through so many different situations over the years, yet through those experiences, I learned how to be a father of steel and velvet.

Isaiah was a kid who constantly sought my approval. Anytime I would become upset with him, he didn't' rest until we were ok again. He sought to please me in academics as well as in sports, but he struggled to learn that pleasing God was more important. God delivered Isaiah from an unsafe environment to one that afforded him opportunity to attend college and receive a scholarship in track and field.

I recall when he left for college; I left him with the admonishment to stay focused in school, make good decisions, and to be committed to his Christian values. My wife and I moved him into his dorm on a Sunday afternoon. After making sure he had everything he needed, we prayed, embraced him, and traveled home. Leaving Isaiah was difficult for me. Although I wanted him to pursue his college goals and enjoy the college experience, the house had some sense of emptiness and part of me wished he was there. I knew, however, that he was in God's hands and I had taught him what was necessary for him to be successful. The following Saturday, only six days after we had dropped Isaiah off, I received a phone call from him. I could tell by the tone of his voice that he was very nervous. He proceeded to tell me that the previous night, he received a call from some guys he had just met on campus. The guys were at a club, had been drinking, and wanted him to come to the club to drive them home. In a naive attempt to establish friendship, Isaiah agreed and walked to the club to pick the boys up and their car. Unfortunately, on his way back to campus, he was pulled over by the police because the right turn signal on the car he was driving, which was not his own, was not working. After receiving a traffic ticket for the violation, he returned knowing this was not the way to start his new college experience.

When Isaiah shared this with me I was very angry. Just six days prior, I had told him what my expectations were, and already he broke the rules. Why would he walk at 2 A.M in the morning, alone in a new city, and then drive someone else's car he barley knew? These are the questions I asked myself in frustration as I paced the backyard for the next hour while talking to God. Although it may seem like a minimal offense, I knew that unless Isaiah began making better decisions, he would have many struggles to come.

As I continued my pace, I asked God what He wanted me to do. God answered. "Go get him." I admit, I was surprised at God's answer. However, if God wanted me to go get him, that's what I would do. I called Isaiah back and informed him that he needed to pack all of his stuff and be ready because we were on our way back down to get him, and he was to enroll at the local junior college that following Monday. Perhaps Isaiah wasn't ready to be away at college.

My wife and I made the journey once again, picked him up, and brought him back home. Needless to say, Isaiah was upset and disappointed in this decision. On the ride back home, I wondered if I was too harsh...did I really hear that God wanted me to bring him back home? Perhaps I was just angry and making too much of nothing. I began questioning my discipline. That evening we didn't really discuss much. I was exhausted from the trip and told him we would discuss it the next day. I prayed and asked God to give me an answer the next morning. If He wanted me to let him go back or keep him at home I would do whatever He desired.

As I awoke that next morning, God gave me His answer. We returned Isaiah to college that same afternoon. God wanted him to understand the standard that was set and how important it was to adhere to it. Isaiah had to understand that he couldn't take God's blessings for granted else they might be forfeited. I was a very steel father that Saturday afternoon by making him move back, but I was velvet the next day as I told him how much I loved him and allowed him to go back.

Chapter 4: Steel and Velvet

As I experience life, I find that there are many things that challenge me in all aspects such as my character, integrity, and commitment to God. I recall a time in my childhood years when I disobeyed my father. His response to my disobedience was with love yet sternness. I suffered a hard physical consequence, but it set me back on the right track and reminded me of whom I was and what I was supposed to be. Throughout my childhood, my father often taught me how to be an honest person even through dishonest moments. My very character is attributed to what he sowed in me. His moments of "steel" were necessary so that his moments of "velvet" would be appreciated. You must show love and discipline just as God disciplines you according to Hebrews 12:4-11 (NIV):

In your struggle against sin, you have not yet resisted to the point of shedding your blood. ⁵ And have you completely forgotten this word of encouragement that addresses you as a father addresses his son? It says,

"My son, do not make light of the Lord's discipline,
and do not lose heart when he rebukes you,
⁶ because the Lord disciplines the one he loves,
and he chastens everyone he accepts as his son."[a]

⁷ Endure hardship as discipline; God is treating you as his children. For what children are not disciplined by their father? ⁸ If you are not disciplined—and everyone undergoes discipline—then you are not legitimate, not true sons and daughters at all. ⁹ Moreover, we have all had human fathers who disciplined us and we respected them for it. How much more should we submit to the Father of spirits and live! ¹⁰ They disciplined us for a little while as they thought best; but God disciplines us for our good, in order that we may share in his holiness. ¹¹ No discipline seems pleasant at the time, but painful. Later on, however, it produces a harvest of righteousness and peace for those who have been trained by it.

If you are committed to be *somewhere in between*, you must possess the ability to be steel and velvet. There is a delicate balance that must take place in order to raise young men to be highly respected men of God. Too much steel breeds a hard, unemotional, and impatient person. Men who are mostly steel don't show emotion well and often struggle with outward affection. Too much velvet breeds passive men who often struggle to stand up for what they believe. Purely velvet men are afraid of confrontation and will often agree with things in order to avoid upsetting someone. A proper balance of these two types of men is the necessary recipe for raising Christian young men to posses the same attributes.

I became involved with raising a young man that was 11-years-old who had a very troubled background. I spent the next several years teaching, caring for, nurturing, and guiding him throughout high school. I once again found myself *somewhere in between*, but this time my commitment would be tested and my patience pressed. Surprisingly, high school went well. I can only recall two incidents that I received a call from a school administrator, both of which were minor offenses. Senior year, however, I began to notice a change in character that would soon negatively change our relationship. When he turned 18, he adopted the "I'm a grown man" attitude and decided that he no longer had to consult my wife or me on anything; rather could do whatever he wanted. I began to see rebellion, disrespect, and a lack of appreciation for what he had been given for the last seven years. After all, for so long I was simply *somewhere in between*. I set aside my own agenda and followed the direction of God when I decided to take care of him. Had he forgotten that I wasn't required to sacrifice so much? As time went on, our relationship continued to decline and he eventually moved out to stay with a friend. I watched him change from a trusting and respectful young man, to one that would lie often and be highly disrespectful to myself and others.

What happened in his life that changed him so dramatically? This is the question I asked of God, who revealed to me the spiritual nature of the situation and revealed it to me though the example of the Prodigal son:

Jesus continued: "There was a man who had two sons. The younger one said to his father, 'Father, give me my share of the estate.' So he divided his property between them.

"Not long after that, the younger son got together all he had, set off for a distant country and there squandered his wealth in wild living. After he had spent everything, there was a severe famine in that whole country, and he began to be in need. So he went and hired himself out to a citizen of that country, who sent him to his fields to feed pigs. He longed to fill his stomach with the pods that the pigs were eating, but no one gave him anything.
Luke 15:11-16(NIV)

The key element in this scripture is that the prodigal son selfishly squandered his wealth in wild living in a far off country. This was parallel to what was going on with this young man whom

I was raising. The "property" referred to in the scripture was not just material things. The prodigal was given responsibility, wisdom, and spiritual awareness, all of which were far more valuable than material wealth; however, he wasted it all and did not put to use these values. He soon found himself living worse than the servants in his father's house and was faced with a decision to either continue on his own or return to his father.

It was the steel in his father that gave him his inheritance and allowed him to venture out on his own. His father saw beginning in him what so many young men go through, which is the desire to prematurely "grow up" and "become men." His son equated taking care of himself with manhood. Although the ability to take care of oneself is indeed a character of manhood, unless one is ready, it can lead to disaster.

God revealed to me a tremendous parallel between the prodigal son and this young man. All his life the prodigal son was given so much. He lived in the best of places, he was clothed in the finest of clothes, and always had good food to eat. He took for granted the hard work that his father had put into providing these things for him. Although his father did not agree, he did not hinder his son from leaving. He remained strong, dealt with his son as a man, and sent him on his way. Of course his heart was troubled, and his spirit was heavy, but he trusted that God would look after his son each night and day when he no longer could.

God himself is a god of steel and velvet. There are times that His servants get off track and begin living outside of His will and His purpose. It is God's mercy, however, that is velvet, and it is God's love that is steel. As you stand *somewhere in between*, you must mirror the image of God and reflect that image onto the young men whose lives you are given responsibility.

17 "When he came to his senses, he said, 'How many of my father's hired servants have food to spare, and here I am starving to death! 18 I will set out and go back to my father and say to him: Father, I have sinned against heaven and against you. 19 I am no longer worthy to be called your son; make me like one of your hired servants.' 20 So he got up and went to his father.

"But while he was still a long way off, his father saw him and was filled with compassion for him; he ran to his son, threw his arms around him and kissed him.

As you stand *somewhere in between*, there will be moments that you will have to let go and allow God to work on His children. To a man of steel and velvet, this is a difficult task, but you must ask God for understanding and allow Him to have full-control. By letting God take control, you are recognizing God's voice, showing patience and commitment, and understanding that this is God's assignment for you and you are simply a tool in His ministry. The prodigal son came to his senses and returned home. It was the velvet in his father that caused him to show compassion towards his son and greet him with a kiss.

Points to Consider

Chapter 4: Steel and Velvet

- Moments of "steel" are necessary so that the moments of "velvet" are appreciated
- The proper balance of steel and velvet is the necessary recipe for a Christian man
- Moments will come when you have to let go and allow God to work with His children

Somewhere to Write...

How has God shown you "steel?" How has He shown you "velvet?" How can you use your experiences in the lives of those that you are mentoring?

_____

_____

_____

_____

_____

_____

_____

_____

_____

_____

_____

_____

_____

_____

_____

_____

_____

_____

Somewhere to Write...

"And they lifted up their voice, and wept again: and Orpah kissed her mother in law; but Ruth clave unto her."
Ruth 1:14 (KJV)

Paul

When I first met Paul, he was 11-years-old. Our meeting was indirect. I first began mentoring his older brother, and through him, came to know Paul also. He lived in the inner-city, in a low income neighborhood riddled with crime and poverty. Paul's mother and sister were killed in a car accident when he was only a year old. He was also in that same accident, but survived along with two of his older brothers. Paul's father was shot to death, then was burned in his own car. The tragic deaths of both his parents occurred approximately eight months apart. His grandparents then took on the responsibility to raise him and his brothers. Paul had an uphill journey in life from its very start.

After about one year, Paul and I began interacting on a regular basis. He would stay with my family and me religiously every other weekend. He and my youngest son became good friends and soon became like brothers. Paul, however, was troubled and had some academic problems at school. He was very apathetic concerning his education and his grandmother struggled to keep him on track. I had encountered this situation before in my mentoring experience so no problem...or so I thought. As time went on, I became a close family friend and his grandmother gave me full permission to stand in as a father-figure in his life. Although I had the position with Paul and had support from Paul's grandmother, there was something missing. Our relationship lacked the connection that I had felt for others. I knew I was doing a good thing by mentoring Paul, but my spirit didn't feel it. I prayed and asked God for direction, and He gave me my answer. God reminded me that Paul and I meeting was indirect. God had not sent me to Paul or Paul to me, but I had moved forward to mentor him on my own volition. God had not ordained the relationship and it was frustrating and unproductive. I had a difficult task to fulfill ahead. I had to end it.

At the conclusion of one weekend, I decided that I would finally end our relationship. I dropped him off one Sunday afternoon as usual and simply never returned. I never had a conversation with Paul because I was too much of a coward. I never had a conversation with Paul's grandmother for I knew she would be upset and disappointed. I just never picked up the phone to call again, although everyday after that, the thought of Paul never left me. My youngest son still asked about Paul. I felt ashamed that I walked away. Never before had I ever given up on a child. It was my lowest moment in mentoring.

One year went by and the phone rang late one evening. It was Paul. He had lost my number and was calling to see how I had been. The conversation was short; I was cordial and we hung up without making any future plans for reuniting. I still did not feel the Holy Spirit guiding me to Paul. Six more months would go by and I ran into one of Paul's teachers, who was also a member of my church. Paul had been asking about me and that is when God intervened. I gave his teacher my number and asked him to give it to Paul. He called that next night and that same weekend, we reignited our relationship. This time, however, it was different. This time, God had ordained the relationship. Paul and I hadn't seen each other in a year and a half, yet that first weekend felt as if we had never been apart. I was frank with Paul and asked him what he wanted out of our relationship. "A father-son relationship" was his response. I apologized to him for leaving and told him there was no excuse for that. He forgave me and didn't ever think I left him, rather he just lost my number. Although I had been reckless in my attempt to mentor him without God's blessing, God had still protected Paul's heart. I thanked God for that. Over the next several months I began to see progress in Paul's schoolwork. Finally, I was seeing the productivity that lacked before. Through my relationship with Paul, I experienced first-hand the power of God's Word as written in Romans 8:28. Although I had not listened to the voice of God in the first place, He still gave me the opportunity to be *somewhere in between* for Paul and our relationship was stronger than it had ever been. I reflected the love of God and he sought to follow my guidance.

Chapter 5: A Naomi Reflection

Have you ever tried to look through a dirty mirror? How about one that is cracked or tarnished? Seeing a good and true reflection in such a mirror is not only difficult, it's often obscure and misleading to the viewer. However, a mirror that is clear, clean, and spot-free reflects a true image without distortion. The same spot-free reflection holds true for you who are willing to be *somewhere in between*. Every person reflects something; the question is "what?" How you live your life, the vices you have, the language you speak, and the activities in which you engage, all determine what kind of reflection you display. The reflection that you display is seen by the young men that God has placed in your life.

How important is this image? You certainly cannot change what you reflect unless you change the object of the image. Many are fooled into thinking that you can deceive the eyes of those watching you and make them think that what they see is different than reality. I have often heard the phrase "Do as I say, not as I do" or alternately, "Do as you hear, not as you see." This can be as difficult for a child to follow as it would be to try to convince a sheep that it is a wolf. No matter what you tell the sheep, when he looks in the mirror, he still will see wool and horns and he'll never be able to growl!

The men that are *somewhere in between* are challenged to continually polish and maintain their reflection for the good of the young men for whom they are given charge. God gives you a tremendous example of such a Godly reflection in the life of Naomi as found in Ruth 1:1-22.

Naomi was a woman of God who lived in Bethlehem, Judah. She was married and had two sons. At some point, a famine struck the land and there was much struggle. Naomi and her husband decided to leave Bethlehem and move to the country of Moab where they thought life would be a bit easier. The Bible, however, teaches that sometime later, Naomi's husband died and Naomi was left with her two sons. Her sons eventually married Moabite women, one by the name of Orpah, the other Ruth. Many years went by and eventually both of Naomi's sons also died. Seeing that she was left alone, only with her daughters-in-law, and that the famine had ended, she decided it was time to return to Bethlehem. She encouraged Ruth and Orpah to go back to their Moabite families, but they insisted on going back with Naomi to Bethlehem.

As I considered this story, the question is raised throughout, "Why would they want to go with her and not to their Moabite family?" Why was this divine intervention? Naomi was a special woman. God specifically chose her to fulfill a very important role in the ancestry of Jesus Christ. In Matthew 1, Naomi's daughter-in-law Ruth's name is listed in Jesus' ancestry. Just think what might have taken place had Naomi not provided such a remarkable reflection for Ruth. It's conceivable that God would have chosen someone else, but what an honorable opportunity for Naomi to be part of God's divine plan to provide eternal salvation for mankind.

When you, a man of God, stand *somewhere in between*, you too are acting under God's will and ultimately for His eternal purpose. You have a divine opportunity to shape and mold the lives of others. Many times you don't realize God is placing you in key positions in this spiritual warfare so that you can be valuable and influential soldiers in His spiritual army. You must also continue to remember the word of God spoken through Paul in Ephesians 6:10-10.

Finally, be strong in the Lord and in his mighty power. ¹¹Put on the full armor of God so that you can take your stand against the devil's schemes. ¹²For our struggle is not against flesh and blood, but against the rulers, against the authorities, against the powers of this dark world and against the spiritual forces of evil in the heavenly realms.

God desires to use you in His ministry to be reflections for these young men who would otherwise be lost, void of direction, or without focus. You don't know the fullness of the spiritual warfare that Paul speaks about because God has not yet revealed all of these mysteries to you. All you can do is continue to strive to make a formidable impact in the lives of the young men around you.

There is much that can be learned from Ruth and Naomi's relationship that directly relates to your stance of being *somewhere in between*. The book of Ruth's further expounds upon this reflection of Naomi:

"Then she arose with her daughters-in-law, that she might return from the country of Moab: for she had heard in the country of Moab how that the LORD had visited his people in giving them bread. ⁷Wherefore she went forth out of the place where she was, and her two daughters in law with her; and they went on the way to return unto the land of Judah. ⁸And Naomi said unto her two daughters in law, Go, return each to her mother's house: the LORD deal kindly with you, as ye have dealt with the dead, and with me. ⁹The LORD grant you that ye may find

rest, each of you in the house of her husband. Then she kissed them; and they lifted up their voice, and wept. ¹⁰And they said unto her, "Surely we will return with thee unto thy people." ¹¹And Naomi said, "Turn again, my daughters: why will ye go with me? are there yet any more sons in my womb, that they may be your husbands? ¹²Turn again, my daughters, go your way; for I am too old to have an husband. If I should say, I have hope, if I should have a husband also tonight, and should also bear sons;

¹³Would ye tarry for them till they were grown? Would ye stay for them from having husbands? Nay, my daughters; for it grieveth me much for your sakes that the hand of the LORD is gone out against me. ¹⁴And they lifted up their voice, and wept again: and Orpah kissed her mother-in-law; but Ruth clave unto her. ¹⁵And she said, Behold, thy sister-in-law is gone back unto her people, and unto her gods: return thou after thy sister-in-law. ¹⁶And Ruth said, Entreat me not to leave thee, or to return from following after thee: for whither thou goest, I will go; and where thou lodgest, I will lodge: thy people shall be my people, and thy God my God." Ruth 1:6-16(KJV)

Do not mistake Naomi's encouragement for her daughters-in-law to return to their kin in Moab as simple apathy. On the contrary, it is a reminder that Satan is continually attempting to thwart your work for God. Perhaps he was telling Naomi that her daughters-in-law would embarrass her, that she didn't have time to deal with them, and that they certainly were not worth the sacrifice because they were not even her "real" daughters. Has Satan ever attempted to dissuade you that way?

When you stand *somewhere in between*, many times family and friends will question your involvement and level of commitment in the lives of the young men you mentor. Many will discourage you and remind you that you are not their "real" father. They will say that you shouldn't dedicate so much time or have so much concern for the welfare of others. At times you may also be told that certain events or trips are "family only" and be discouraged from including "outsiders." This type of "friendly fire" is common and can leave you wounded with frustration and make you question if your effort is truly worth it. In order to overcome those who discourage you, use your shield of faith as described in Ephesians 6:16:

In addition to all this, take up the shield of faith, with which you can extinguish all the flaming arrows of the evil one.

As long as you have faith in what God is doing through you, even friendly fire will be deflected. As a man of God, it is imperative to remember that God has given you a divine appointment, and the life of the one whom you nurture is precious and important to God. **If you keep your focus on God's will, He will speak to the hearts and minds of those opposing and discouraging you.**

Do you have a reflection so bright and alluring that someone would be willing to go and die with you? Ruth had such conviction, no doubt brought about by Naomi's unconditional love for her. The Holy Bible teaches that it was Naomi's reflection that caused her daughters to cleave to her. As Orpah and Ruth observed their mother-in-law over the years, they must have watched as she was challenged by the famine, as she grieved for her husband and sons, and as she endured many years of hardship and conflict. Through these trials, Naomi reflected God's love, patience, commitment, faith and endurance, day after day. Have you ever wondered what life or situation a young man returns to if not for someone being a true reflection of Christ in his life? Today's society hardly reflects an adequate Godly atmosphere that will and can properly guide youth. If the men that God has chosen don't take position, the youth will return to an empty life and may never reach their full potential. You must stand strong and be reflections of truth, love, and charity as you emulate your Savior Jesus Christ.

Points to Consider

Chapter 5: A Naomi Reflection

- The reflection that you display is seen by the young men that God places in your life
- You have a divine opportunity to shape and mold the lives of others
- Do not be discouraged by "friendly fire" but stay focused on the purpose of God

Somewhere to Write...

What does your reflection look like to the young men you are guiding? Are there things that need to change in order to make it shine? What friendly fire are you encountering today? What are some practical things that you can do to shield the friendly fire?

_____

_____

_____

_____

_____

_____

_____

_____

_____

_____

_____

_____

_____

_____

_____

_____

_____

_____

Somewhere to Write...

_____

_____

_____

_____

_____

_____

_____

_____

_____

_____

_____

_____

_____

_____

_____

_____

_____

_____

_____

_____

_____

_____

_____

"To everything there is a season, and a time to every purpose under heaven."
Ecclesiastes 3:1 (KJV)

Chapter 6: A Balance of Time

One winter day I was going about things as normal, getting my youngest son ready for school, driving to work, and going about the usual workday. Although these activities were necessary, they were just part of my regular routine. It wasn't until late that evening that I realized that my watch had stopped at 2:35 P.M. exactly. How is it that I went through the rest of the day and never once looked at the time? What is the significance of time? In virtually every sport there is a timeout. Most often it's called to review a play to give the coach time to strategize and talk to his team, or it's called due to an injury. Time is used as if it was an infinite substance, and people cling to it like a rare collectible. You get so busy going about your agenda, your day, your activities, and your schedules, that it's easy to forget that time does not belong to you. You race to meetings and rush to meet with friends, almost as if to race against time. On the contrary, much of the day is spent wasting time. You are productive to no one and you serve no worthy purpose. How foolish are you who waste time assuming that you have an abundance?

The men of God that decide to be *somewhere in between* will face the tremendous challenge of balancing time and finding the energy to complete all of your tasks. Your day will demand time and will seem to focus on that very thing. Your wives or significant others, children, church, friends, job, and personal activities will all demand time in your day. It will be imperative that to find success in this challenge by learning the time-balance that God would desire.

The book of Ecclesiastes describes time through such poetry and truth. It implies that time is not a collection of seconds, minutes, hours, days or years, but on the contrary; it is about seasons in which God sets the pace. In Ecclesiastes 3:1-8:

To every thing there is a season, and a time to every purpose under the heaven:

²A time to be born, and a time to die; a time to plant, and a time to pluck up that which is planted;

³A time to kill, and a time to heal; a time to break down, and a time to build up;

⁴A time to weep, and a time to laugh; a time to mourn, and a time to dance;

⁵A time to cast away stones, and a time to gather stones together; a time to embrace, and a time to refrain from embracing;

⁶A time to get, and a time to lose; a time to keep, and a time to cast away;

⁷A time to rend, and a time to sew; a time to keep silence, and a time to speak;

⁸A time to love, and a time to hate; a time of war, and a time of peace.

As I have stood *somewhere in between* for so many young men, a common question asked by others is "How do you have time to take care of all these boys?" The honest answer is that God has taught me balance. It is an incredible challenge to maintain a marriage, endure the responsibilities of a job, handle the responsibility of being a minister, and raise children. I've had my share of disagreements with my wife regarding time and attention, and reprimands at the job for leaving early to attend a sporting event or tutoring session. Also, I have many late nights where I took a walk through the neighborhood or sat on the porch just to have a few minutes of personal time. Balancing time among all the things in life for which you are given responsibility can only be done by prioritizing time, throwing away your agenda, and focusing on God's agenda.

There are four categories that will demand your time and are to be considered in this order of priority:

1. God
2. Wife
3. Children
4. Job and Personal Endeavors

God

God is a jealous god (Exodus 34:14). Often life gets so filled with kids, job, and personal activities that God is placed last on the list. He desires, however, to be first in your life and wants you to always depend on Him for everything you need. Standing *somewhere in between means* you trust and depend on God so that you will be spiritually connected with God. It is then that God will direct the path for you and the young men you guide. (Proverbs 3:5,6)

Wife

God is pleased by those who obey His word in respect to their wives. A wife is a man's helpmate and should be honored with love and respect (Hebrews 5:25-28). How well wives are shown love and respect is directly related to your success of being able to stand *somewhere in between*. It is vital for wives to be given time. Be careful not to isolate her and not to neglect her needs. She is a gift from God and should be treated as such. You must remember that you trust in God to speak to your wife and give her understanding as you stand *somewhere in between*. Give her time, love, and respect and allow God to reveal to her your purpose.

Children

When you stand *somewhere in between*, jealousy can arise between your children and the children that God brings your way. Just as with God and your wife, you must also give your own children personal time. The premise of *somewhere in between* is to be more than a mentor and more like a father. The proper way to accomplish this, in respect to time, is to simply intertwine your children with those for whom you're standing *somewhere in between*. This will allow them to feel just as important and loved, and they in turn will accept and respect your position in the lives of the young men. You must remember they too are under your instruction and they must not be forgotten, but teach them also as God instructs. (Ephesians 6:4)

Job and Personal Endeavors

Jobs and personal endeavors consume much of your time on a daily basis. A significant amount of this time is spent on these things and far too often they overshadow your children, wife, and most of all, God. If not careful, you will unknowingly build your foundation on these things and forsake God's ministry. It is then that what you have built is at risk to be destroyed. (I Corinthians 3:11-15). A key to balancing time is to simply take the young men that you are guiding with you. Be careful not to create "sideline ministries" or get outside of your normal routine. God will bring those into your life that will be able to flow with you as you flow with Him. It can be tempting to create special activities and outings in an effort to provide entertainment. Although this may seem like a good thing, it does not have a spiritual focus and can distract from God's purpose. Mentoring programs that focus on engaging youth in activities have their benefits, but also have limited use. More is "caught than taught" and there are more teachable moments in day-to-day interaction than planned, sporadic interactions.

If time is balanced effectively, and properly prioritized, you can put away your agenda and follow God's agenda. Even if your watch stops, you will be unaware because your focus will be on God and not your own personal desires. Once time is balanced and a foundation is built on God, success of standing *somewhere in between* will be accomplished in a miraculous way. Unless you have a solid foundation of God, all other things you build your life on will be like sinking sand (Matthew 7:26,27).

Points to Consider:

Chapter 6: Balance of Time:

- God is the first priority and is to be given adequate time
- Your foundation must be built on God
- You must understand that your agenda is irrelevant and God's agenda should be prevalent

Somewhere to Write...

What daily activities take most of your time? How much of that time belongs to God? What challenges with balancing time have you encountered since standing *somewhere in between?*

_____

_____

_____

_____

_____

_____

_____

_____

_____

_____

_____

_____

_____

_____

_____

_____

_____

_____

_____

_____

Devin E. Caruthers

Somewhere to Write...

_____

_____

_____

_____

_____

_____

_____

_____

_____

_____

_____

_____

_____

_____

_____

_____

_____

_____

_____

_____

_____

"For there stood by me this night the angel of God, whose I am, and whom I serve, Saying, Fear not, Paul; thou must be brought before Caesar: and, lo, God hath given thee all them that sail with thee." Acts 27:23 KJV

David

David liked to learn things the hard way. Instead of listening, he would often insist on doing his own thing against my better judgment or even despite logical thought. Most of his teenage years were spent wandering though life, ignoring directions at times, and diverting from the main path. God, however, saw that David was going to get lost and provided for him a spiritual guide through me. At this particular time, I was yet still learning that God was not only placing me in the lives of many to teach and encourage them, but He was also giving me spiritual direction for their lives.

In the Book of Acts, Paul is sailing for Italy as a prisoner to stand trial before Caesar. In Acts 27:10, he *perceives* the voyage will bring "hurt and much damage" to the landing, the ship and even the lives of all on board. During my interaction with David, God helped me to perceive things to come just as Paul did. David, however, responded just as those on the ship did with Paul. He ignored my admonishments and proceeded to live his life regardless of my warnings.

By the time David finished high school, he had climbed to much success as an athlete. He was highly recruited by an area university to run track and quickly began breaking school records his freshman year in college. David, however, did not deal well with his success. Instead of giving God the glory as I had taught him, he instead credited himself with his success. He became arrogant, prideful, and cocky, lacking all humility in most of what he did. David thought that he should be at a better university, forgetting that it was God that placed him there in the first place. I warned David, that if he didn't keep his eyes on God, stay focused in school, and appreciate what God had given him, he would forfeit his blessing and suffer great loss. Unfortunately, David continued his life of disrespect, misdirection, and dishonor of God through irresponsible and sinful living.

God spoke to me and gave me a scripture for David; I Peter 5:5-10. He made me spiritually aware that because of David's lack of humility and obedience to His Word, he would suffer and lose all of what God had given him. On three occasions I sent this scripture to David, and each time he did not read it. Over the course of six months, God made good on his warning and repossessed David's blessings. He no longer had a track scholarship or was even on the track team. He also lost his car, his money, his friends, and most importantly, his position and favor with God. It was very difficult to watch David live life with so many disregards to what God had done for him. It was even more difficult to see it coming yet have no power to change it. Despite the circumstances, I was there to help him pick up the pieces and guide him back to his path. After all, God chose me to be David's spiritual guide and I am thankful to Him for the assignment.

Chapter 7: Spiritually Aware

Late one night, in the spring of 1999, I found myself standing outside my car looking up at the sky; my soul crying out to God. My world felt like it had been turned upside-down and nothing I did seemed to right my situation. Those trials and tribulations that I had heard about in so many testimonies at church surely became weights in my life. My heart seemed to speak before my lips uttered a word and it was in anguish over many problems that I faced. My eyes filled with tears and my spirit was heavy; I had come to this place for an answer from God. For the first time in my life, I questioned if God was truly a present help as His Word testified. I remember the night suddenly falling still, as if God Himself had hushed all creation just to listen to me. As I poured out my heart, I asked God to make His presence known with a sign. In a moment, God ordered His wind to encircle me in a strong, but comforting, whirlwind. Although it only lasted for a few moments, that was the defining moment in my spiritual awareness. It awakened me to God's magnificent presence and confirmed for me that He indeed listens to the prayers of His children.

Spiritual awareness is vitally important if you are willing to stand *somewhere in between*. This is not just another mentoring program with earthly goals and agendas. On the contrary, it is a God-ordained ministry, and if you accept the call into it, you must understand that "*in between*" is where God has placed you. If you step out of position, you will not effectively influence the lives of those God has placed under your direction. To completely understand the importance of your spiritual awareness, look at the historical account of the Apostle Paul in the book of Acts.

Paul was a prisoner aboard a ship, traveling to Rome to stand trial before Caesar. As he, the other prisoners, and the guards journeyed along the shore of Crete, a storm with wind of hurricane force swept down and caused the ship to change course.

[21]After the men had gone a long time without food, Paul stood up before them and said: "Men, you should have taken my advice not to sail from Crete; then you would have spared yourselves this damage and loss. [22]But now I urge you to keep up your courage, because not one of you will be lost; only the ship will be destroyed. [23]Last night an angel of the God whose I am and whom I serve stood beside me [24]and said, 'Do not be afraid, Paul. You must stand trial before Caesar; and God has graciously given you the lives of all who sail with you.' [25]So keep up your courage, men, for I have faith in God that it will happen just as he told me. [26]Nevertheless, we must run aground on some island." Acts 27:21-26(NIV)

As a byproduct to standing *somewhere in between* for young men, often times you will say things and you won't be heard, you'll give advice that won't be heeded, and you'll give direction that won't be followed. If you are aware that you have a spiritual position in their lives, it will encourage you to continue guiding them, for they will indeed get in trouble at times and lose their way. Being "*somewhere in between*" is representative of the ship, and all of the young men God places in your life are representative of the other people onboard the ship. The awesome reality is that because men of God, like you, that are positive influences, cause the lives of so many young men to be spared, and allow them unimaginable opportunities. Paul had a destination and so do you. Simply because you are onboard, God's grace covers your passengers! God is speaking to all who are courageous and willing to hear His voice. He reminds you to not be afraid of the challenge that He has set before you.

If you accept the command to stand *somewhere in between*, you cannot be afraid to raise someone else's child. Just as Paul, you must have faith in God and continue to stand in the gap until God's purpose is fulfilled. The historical account of Paul's journey teaches so much if you are willing to learn. It is important to note that the ship did not make it safely to Rome. On the contrary, it did succumb to the violence of the waves, and the strength of the wind, and the ship was broken into pieces while still off shore. You must realize that every assignment God gives you is not permanent. As Paul journeyed on this ship, God entrusted the lives of more than 200 prisoners and guards to his direction, but only for a season. When Paul fulfilled his divine obligation, his journey continued without them. As you stand in position, the Holy Spirit will speak to you and give you specific and unique direction for each of the lives that you will touch. After your journey with each young man is complete, God may move you on and possibly give you yet another one of His children that needs someone to be *somewhere in between*.

Points to Consider

Chapter 7: Spiritually Aware

- Spiritual awareness is vitally important in understanding your position
- Your presence in the lives of young men extends them spiritual grace from God
- Every assignment may not be permanent and may only be for a season

Somewhere to Write...

How has the grace of God helped you in your life? How can it be extended to those that you are mentoring? Is God telling you a season is coming to an end?

_____

_____

_____

_____

_____

_____

_____

_____

_____

_____

_____

_____

_____

_____

_____

_____

_____

_____

Somewhere to Write...

_____

_____

_____

_____

_____

_____

_____

_____

_____

_____

_____

_____

_____

_____

_____

_____

_____

_____

_____

_____

_____

_____

Getting Started

The easiest way for you to become *somewhere in between* is to get involved with the youth in your community. I encourage you to become a volunteer in your church's youth group, coach sports, or perhaps become a tutor. Take advantage of every opportunity to be involved with youth. As you make yourself available, the Holy Spirit will begin to speak to you and guide you to the young person that he desires for you to provide positive influence. If you recognize God's voice and respond to His command, you will be added to the family of God's men who stand *somewhere in between* in the lives of many.

Scripture and Statement of Commitment

Religion that God our Father accepts as pure and faultless is this: to look after orphans and widows in their distress and to keep oneself from being polluted by the world.
James 1:27 (NIV)

I _____ commit to stand *somewhere in between* for whomever God sends my way. I pledge to listen to God, be committed to God's purpose, patient, a man of steel and velvet, exhibit a Naomi reflection, balance my time effectively, and be a spiritually aware man of God.

Signature _____

Date_____

Addendum

Letters to My Father

The following letters are personal reflections of five young men that God placed in my life for me to be *somewhere in between*. The life story of each is unique and each of them has faced many challenges. The grace of God, however, gave them new life and focuses, and provided them a great opportunity to be successful men of God. These letters were written to me from their hearts as an expression of appreciation and love. It is my desire that when you read their letters, you will understand the importance and tremendous impact you can have by standing *somewhere in between* in the lives of young men.

Letter #1

Dear Goddaddy,

This part of my life is not yet complete. But as each day of my life goes on, I see us coming closer and closer together. At one point in time, my father was my world, but as I got older, things started to change. I felt as if me and my father started to lose connection. I couldn't understand why. I searched for an answer but there was none. Sometimes I would cry, but I soon realized that I would have to move on. That's where you, my God Dad, came in my life. At first I didn't know how to react, so I kind of stayed to myself, giving you parts of my life as time went on and then you wanted to stay. We started with building a father/son relationship and moved on from there. You have done so much for me. You direct my life in a different direction. You were there for me at times when I felt there was no one there. Now where we stand is amazing. We have this connection to where we both know when something is bothering us. You are truly the father I've always wanted, knowing how you came in my life and what you've done even though you don't have to show me that you have and that you love me. The time you spend on me when you could be doing anything else I thank you for. You're always there for me no matter what it is, and when I'm sick you won't rest until you know I'm better; although we're not in the same place, it still feels as if you're there. I love you as a father. You have changed my life completely, teaching me right from wrong, showing me talents about myself that I didn't know I had and teaching me how to become a man. I have learned a lot and there's still more to come.

Love you,

Your favorite son

Letter #2

Dear Daddy,

First I would like to start by saying thanks for being in my life. There are many kids that would love to have someone in their life that inspires me the way that you do. You inspire me not just spiritually, but also in ways such as becoming a man, teaching me how to treat others, and most of all how to treat the ones that you love. Growing up years before meeting you, I never thought about college or even high school for that matter. The only thing that was on my mind was getting money anyway that I can and as fast I can. You taught me that I will appreciate the things that I have if I got it the proper way by working for what I want. I had never thought there was a way that I would be happy when I wake up in the morning, not worrying about if I was going to eat today or what did I have to do to eat. The day that you told me that I could come live with you was the happiest day of my life; I still see your face bright as all get out and I knew from there that you genuinely care about me and my future. You have taught and done so many things for me throughout my life I really don't know how I can pay you back. You always say, "Your pay back to me is to graduate from college." Yes, that can be true, but that to me doesn't compare to what you have done for me. I would like to say thank you and love you and I thank God everyday that he has placed you in my life. I could only imagine what the world would be if it was filled with men with the same heart that you have.

Love your son

Letter #3

Dear Dado,

Where do I start? You have been that father figure that a kid without a father only hoped for. You were the person that took me under your wing when I had no one there to count on, whether it was for something to eat or just to give me something to do during the day. It started when I was in the fourth grade when we first met; you became the Field Elementary School basketball coach. When we first met, my brother and I were lost. We didn't know which way to turn but you instantly became someone that we could count on. You took us to the arcade, the mall and the park to work on our basketball game, but throughout all of those things I noticed that you were teaching us day by day on how to become young and respectful young men at the time. This is something that only a man could do for a young boy and not any man could just raise a child. You need guidance from above and this brings me to how you always taught us no matter what happens in life always BELIEVE that GOD does those things for a reason and I found myself to truly believe that. Now that I am an adult ,and I look at all the things that I couldn't have been doing in my life with the way that I was going, I am grateful that I can do other things. With the right guidance I have been able to participate in track, football and various other opportunities that have come about. I have been to several different places that I would not have been able to go to if my life didn't take the right turns and I was given that second chance to be something in my life.

Love you

Letter #4

My Dad...
My dad was always there when I had trouble,
And if I needed him he was coming on the double.
But then we lost contact and everything changed,
And I didn't know what to do,
I lost it.
I went insane.
But God has a reason for everything that He does,
Even if it meant me losing my closest friend
over something stupid such as drugs.
So many things happened over these two years,
I haven't told anyone about because
it would only hurt their ears.
But now at least we have each other again,
And promise that you'll surround
me with your love and care,
Because a relationship like ours is very rare.
As you help me walk up the stairs to success,
I want everyone to know that you Dad are the best.
I love you Dad.

Letter #5

Dear Goddad,

I remember when I first met you. It was at my track meet in the summer of 2009. I had just eaten a hotdog and was walking back to my tent when you walked up to me to introduce yourself. We had a general conversation and you told me that you liked how I ran. I remember telling you that I needed a trainer so you volunteered and at that point my life changed. I love you and you have really changed my life. I just never got around telling you that you're a great man and a great father figure. You have done a lot for me and I hope this book you have taken the time to write will help anyone that takes interest in kids; primarily teens like me. I really don't think I would be where I'm at without you and you even continue to push me to this day. Although we've had our ups and downs it has always came out good and EVERYONE has problems and issues that need to be handled. I know that all this really couldn't have happened without GOD guiding you into my life. Also, because you are a minister you have opened my eyes and turned me back to God.

Thank you lots Goddad, I really appreciate you.

"The Substitute" Preview

The Holy Spirit woke me around 3 A.M. The previous day had been one of the most challenging times standing *somewhere in between*. As I struggled to fall back to sleep, I received an unction from the Holy Spirit to record the emotions of that day in a poem, similar to that of Solomon when writing the Book of Ecclesiastes. "The Substitute," referring to a substitute teacher, provides an analogy to standing *somewhere in between* in lives of those who resent your assignment. As you stand in position as "father," you will often be viewed as just a "substitute." Similar to how substitute teachers are treated in school: disrespected, unappreciated, and resented, you too will often endure the same. You are standing *somewhere in between*, however, to save their life and do something that is vitally important, more important than they'll realize. The Substitute is a poetic illustration inspired by my experience of standing *somewhere in between* for Marcus as mentioned prior to Chapter 2. I encourage you to command your class, teach God's lessons, and graduate your students.

The Substitute

Class is now in session,
The sub got the message late.
Please get out your notebooks
Write this down.
Can someone tell me what the teacher was teaching?
So it's known where to begin.
No lesson plans left,
What was the homework?
Write this down.
Please pay attention,
Why does everything have to be said more than once?
Attendance needs to be taken...
Who is present?
Or perhaps, who is absent?
Selfishness..."Here,"
Anger..."Here,"
Resentment..."Upfront."
Who threw the paper?
The sub is trying to teach.
The class is not paying attention,
There's so much to cover.
Write this down.
The sub is doing the best job possible,
They got the assignment late.
It's known this is not the sub's class,
And a temporary assignment it may be.
"MY FAVORITE TEACHER,"
The sub won't use that mug,
Evil looks from the class even moving it across the desk.

Write this down.

This apple wasn't brought for the sub to enjoy,

The class didn't know there would be a change in plans.

It's reading time,

Class, please get into a circle.

Who called the sub that name?

Who put gum in the chair?

Class, please be respectful,

The sub is doing the best job possible.

Write this down.

A hand rises to ask a question,

"When will the regular teacher return?"

No answer could be given.

No message left, no note, no clue.

The sub will do the best job possible,

No slackin' will take place.

"No thanks," from the class,

"We will wait."

Write this down.

With a heavy heart the sub gazed,

And eyes filled with tears the sub stood,

And with a crackle in his voiced uttered,

"Class dismissed."

The class then waited,

Not sure what to do next.

Still no sign of their teacher,

No message left, no note, no clue.

A student noticed a piece of paper under the desk,

For it was left by the sub in haste.

"Lessons for Today" it read,

The class was listening now.

Lesson #1...Sacrifice,

Lesson #2...Unconditional Love,

Lesson #3...Gratitude,

Lesson #4...Unselfishness,

Lesson #5...Commitment.

This must have been the "so much to cover,"

The sub had planned to teach.

It was based on those absent that day,

In hopes they might return.

The sub has now departed,

Only a sub they ever were.

Although they taught as passionate as the teacher,

They could never take their place.

But there's so much to cover,

And time is going fast.

The class must learn the material,

Just in order to pass.

The sub taught with every part of their heart,

The class laughed and slept.

But the lesson was important,

The class wouldn't receive.

Bits and pieces they would remember,

But would the lesson be lost?

Write this down.

The sub stood alone,

It's time to take a test.

...But no one had a pencil.

But remember, seven times the class

was asked to, "Write it down,"

But, "You're just a substitute."

"Now close my teacher's book,

Get out of their chair,
Erase you name off their board,
And leave the room."
The sub looked around with sadness,
They had tried so hard.
It seemed that everyone felt this way,
And there were no more lessons to be given.
The sub collected a coat, a bag, and a key.
Never to use the special mug,
Or sit in the special chair.
Never to read the special storybook,
Or eat the special fruit.
No sub ever would.
The class sat quietly after hearing the lesson plan,
Now no teacher present to teach at all.
The fruit will rot,
The class will grow older,
And what would they do at grading time?
The sub actually taught those lessons all throughout the day,
Although the class mistreated him,
He taught his heart out anyway.
For he had sacrificed his time to try to fill the spot,
Unconditional love and commitment shown
through every paper thrown.
Through name calling the sub still showed
gratitude to be allowed to stay this long,
Only a substitute they were,
But deeply valued their position.
No more lessons, no more writing.
Class dismissed.

About the Author

James 1:27 lays the premise for my life's purpose. In the summer of 2004, I accepted God's call to the ministry while working in the basement of my first home. God used my ability to build walls to inspire me to build in the lives of others. By the time I entered the ministry, I was already heavily involved, through mentoring, in the lives of many young men. I had the opportunity to experience many of their successes as well as many of their setbacks. It was in that summer that God called me out of the basement, bestowed on me a vision, and placed me on a path that would take His ministry to the highest level.

I have spent the last 12 years pouring myself into the lives of others, especially young men. It was important for me to teach them positive moral values and model how to seed their relationship with Jesus Christ. Many people expect my childhood story to be one of distress and hardship because often times that's what inspires people to care so much. The assumption is that I also grew up fatherless and therefore experienced my own struggles. These assumptions, however, hold no truth. So, where is the source of my passion? I have such a strong passion for the fatherless not because I too grew up without my own but rather the opposite. My father was very present and active in my life. I recall many bonding moments in the backyard or at the kitchen table. He was always there, teaching and guiding me along the way. It was through these moments that I came to understand his importance in my life and his significance and influences radiate in much of who I am. I give so freely because I was given so bountifully. It was my father's presence and influence that fostered the passion for me to look after others in the same manner. When I realized how important he is and was in my life, I could not imagine a life without a father like him. God used my experience to bring out the desire in me to pour into others what my father so graciously and unselfishly poured into me. I believe that every child deserves to feel and experience that same love, a father's love. It was by the grace of God that I was able to grow up with my father as an active and positive presence in my life. In I Corinthians 15:10 the Apostle Paul wrote:

But by the grace of God I am what I am, and his grace to me was not without effect. No, I worked harder than all of them – yet not I, but the grace of God that was with me.

Just as Paul did, I made a commitment to God to work tirelessly in the lives of others. I thank God, my wife, my children, and the countless young men that gave me the inspiration to write this book. It is a reflection of their spiritual journeys and is inspired by God. I pray that it will encourage, motivate, and stimulate men around the world to become *somewhere in between* in the lives of others.